HOLY TANGO

~~ANTHOLOGY~~

of

LITERATURE

HOLY TANGO

of LITERATURE

by FRANCIS HEANEY

illustrated by Richard Thompson

emmis humor

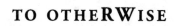
TO OTHERWISE

emmis humor

An insubordinate subdivision of Emmis Books

The Old Firehouse 1700 Madison Road
Cincinnati, OH 45206

www.emmisbooks.com/humor

Portions of this book were originally published, some in slightly different form, on the Modern Humorist Web site and in the anthology *More Mirth of a Nation: The Best Contemporary Humor*.

Library of Congress Cataloging-in-Publication Data

Heaney, Francis, 1970-
Holy tango of literature / by Francis Heaney.
      p. cm.
ISBN 1-57860-159-2
1. Parodies. 2. Anagrams. I. Title.
PN6110.P3H43 2004
808.8—dc22

                                          2004052758

Manufactured in the United States of America
Cover and book design by Gregory Hischak

First Edition
10 9 8 7 6 5 4 3 2 1

best left To Canon
TABLE of CONTENTS

HOLY TANGO

Preface to the First Edition

THE QUESTION of what would happen if poets and playwrights wrote works whose titles were anagrams of their names is one that has been insufficiently studied in the past. This may simply be because most poets and playwrights have not written any works whose titles are anagrams of their names. So, much as musical scholars used Beethoven's unfinished notes to complete his posthumous tenth symphony, we have created a series of literary reconstructions that represent our best guesses as to what such anagram-based literature would be like. Given that we had no notes whatsoever upon which to base our work, we had to be extra scrupulous.

Critics may argue that the works contained in these pages include numerous anachronisms. Our response is that if even the great Shakespeare could include a chiming clock in *Julius Caesar* and a Mickey Mouse doll in *Pericles*, then we should be allowed some leeway as well.

Further, the sharp-eyed reader will note that the titles of works by ancient and foreign authors (such as Chaucer, Bashō, and Euripides) have been translated into modern English. This was done partly as an aid to comprehension, but mostly to prevent us from having to anagram in Middle English, Japanese, or ancient Greek. We may be somewhat obsessive-compulsive, but even we have limits.

Unlike most literary textbooks, this volume is not arranged chronologically or thematically. We feel this approach rewards the casual browser, offering juxtapositions that one would not find in a more traditional collection. Also, it's very expensive to rearrange the pages of a book once they've been typeset.

This book would not have been possible without the aid of many people. We would like to thank Rose White, Daniel Radosh, Randy Cohen, John Aboud, Michael Colton, Trip Payne, Kevin Wald, Ken Stern, and Michael J. Rosen for their assistance, support, advice, and, in Rose's case, sexual prowess.

—*Francis Heaney*

PREFACE TO THE
SECOND EDITION

WE HAVE RECEIVED many queries since the first edition of this anthology was published. Some have asked us why we chose to include scenes from plays instead of printing the full texts. This is a good question. In our defense, we can only say that plays are long. Much longer than poems! We may yet attempt to reconstruct the full-length versions of these plays, however, if the MacArthur Foundation ever ponies up some cash.

Many more readers pointed out a glaring omission from the previous edition—the lack of a comprehensive history of the anagram—which we are delighted to have the opportunity to rectify.

Since the dawn of time, man has anagrammed things. Before there was written language, primitive man would anagram sticks. Some have postulated that a particularly enthusiastic anagram session led to the discovery of fire, and when I say "some," it is entirely possible that I am referring to people whom I have made up, because "some" is such a delightfully ambiguous word. We may never know.

Certainly, though, the development of language was a turning point in the evolution of the anagram. The earliest practitioners of language-based anagrams would take the letters of a word and rearrange them, but would rearrange them to form the same word, switching the two A's in "salad," for example. Fortunately, as language increased in complexity, so did anagrams.

Many cultures ascribed mystical powers to anagrams. When the Ancient Greeks discovered that "Socrates" would one day, in a transliteration to a language that did not yet exist, be anagrammable to the word "coarsest," they immediately had him poisoned. Or so we're told. We haven't checked. Literature is kind of more our thing than history.

Today, anagrams have infiltrated every part of modern society, from puzzle magazines to . . . you name it. What does the future hold for anagrams? Only time will tell.

[Five minutes later]
Still waiting to find out about the anagrams. We may have to wait longer.

—*F. H.*

PREFACE TO THE
THIRD EDITION

THE GOAL of any anthology such as this is to provide a thorough picture of literature through the ages. Accordingly, we have attempted to include works by every major author whose name anagrammed into something vaguely humorous. In most literary anthologies, the hardest decisions involve deciding who to leave out. In our case, it was easy. No decent anagrams? To hell with them. Obviously, other criteria were involved (i.e., "Can I stand to read poetry by this person long enough to write a parody of him or her?"), but we still believe this collection accurately depicts what the world would be like if poets and playwrights were even geekier than they already are.

This edition has been expanded from previous editions, in that this edition exists and previous ones do not.

—F. H.

HOLY TANGO

~~ANTHOLOGY~~

of

LITERATURE

ToilEtS
T. S. Eliot

Let us go then, to the john,
Where the toilet seat waits to be sat upon
Like a lover's lap perched upon ceramic;
Let us go, through doors that do not always lock,
Which means you ought to knock
Lest opening one reveal a soul within
Who'll shout, "Stay out! Did you not see my shin,
Framed within the gap twixt floor and stall?"
No, I did not see that at all.
That is not what I saw, at all.

To the stall the people come to go,
Reading an obscene graffito.

We have lingered in the chamber labeled "MEN"
Till attendants proffer aftershave and mints
As we lather up our hands with soap, and rinse.

larS, nbC guard

Carl Sandburg

Door Watcher with the Keys,
Badge Wearer, Bouncer of Kooks,
Greeter of Stars and the Network's ID Checker;
Logy, husky, squinting,
Keeper of the Security Cams.

They tell me you are vengeful and I believe them, for I have seen you
    getting angry when people write fake names on the sign-in sheet.
And they tell me you are lazy and I answer: Yes, it is true I have seen
    men walk freely to the elevator without being cleared.
And they tell me you are heavy and my reply is: On a napkin or
    plate or a *Newsweek* I have seen the dust from powdered donuts.
And having answered so I turn once more to those who sneer at this
    my sentry, and I give them back the sneer and say to them:
Come and show me another sentry with swivel chair spinning so
    glad to have a job with total health and dental.
Flinging his sharpened pencils into the cork of ceiling tiles above,
    here is a broad-necked watchman set thickly before the little soft
    network executives;
Stern as a prime time censor cutting out ass jokes, bovine as a viewer
    sitting through entire infomercials,

Crew-cutted,

Doodling,

Staring,

Humming,

Reading, yawning, rereading,

Down at the desk, coffee cup empty and dry, sleeping at midnight,

Down in the half-lit lobby of NBC sleeping as a stray cat sleeps,

Sleeping even as a bored high school student sleeps in the back of history class,

Snoring and sleeping but ready to wake all the time, and to claim he was only resting his eyes,

Sleeping!

Sleeping the logy, husky, squinting sleep of Lars, half-Swedish, dreaming, proud to be Door Watcher, Badge Wearer, Bouncer of Kooks, Greeter of Stars, and ID Checker for the Network.

roBber Runts
Robert Burns

Wee, sneaky, glowrin, vill'nous thiefies,
O, how ye filch in half a jiffy!
Ye need na fear a lawman's e'e,
      Ye are so little!
An' fool to chase ye, one must be,
      So fast ye scuttle!

But, Pigmies, it is only meet
Your stubby fingers be so fleet:
The furtive schemes o' Midget Men
      Can bare repay
What we lang-legged folk ha' ta'en
      In joy away.

Ay, small ye are, compared wi' me!
Like a dog who hunts the flea,
I scratch! Tho' 'tis to nae avail,
      Who has it worse?
I'd rather still be slow an' tall,
      An' lose a purse!

MULTICOLORED ARGYLE SEA
SAMUEL TAYLOR COLERIDGE

It is an ancient Mariner,
And he taketh lots of drugs,
And he thinks his beard is made of snakes
And his body crawls with bugs.

He spies a wayward Wedding-Guest,
And pulls the man aside.
"Unhand me! Surely thou art mad,
Thy pupils are so wide."

He holds him with his twitchy stare—
"There was a boat," quoth he.
The Wedding-Guest stands frozen there
Without the will to flee.

"A multicolored argyle sea
Was where our trip began,
We sailed o'er oceans deep and wide
And measureless to man.

And then the winds did drive us on
Into a hidden river,
Where sirens' voices called with songs
To make a stout man shiver.

The trees there all bore tangerines,
To save us from the scurvy.
The sky was of an orange hue,
And things seemed topsy-turvy.

Flowers towered in the sky,
The sunlight showing through;
A green and yellow light fell on
The lost and dazzled crew.

Held captive by a siren's call
The men were drawn ashore.
Though they felt sure they'd seen her face,
It seemed she was no more.

At length we came upon a bridge;
A fountain stood nearby,
Where wooden centaurs feasted on
A great marshmallow pie.

And as the centaurs rocked in place
(They could not move to caper),
A host of hansom cabs appeared,
Each one made out of paper.

The drivers beckoned us inside,
And, helpless to resist,
We took our seats; they cracked their whips
And rode into the mist.

The hansoms crackled in the wind,
Grew soggy with the rain—
Just as it seemed they must collapse,
They left us by a train.

The station porters' eyes were dull,
Their skin was plasticine.
We saw reflected in their ties
Our faces, pale and lean.

And then we heard the siren's voice:
It called to us anew!
Beyond the stile she stood and stared
And bid us all come through.

O'er the turnstile each man went,
Clearing it with a leap.
And I too would have followed her,
But that I fell asleep.
When I awoke, I was alone
Upon the argyle deep."

"God's mercy, ancient Mariner—
At least thou didst survive.
'Tis hard your fellow crew was lost
With none but thee alive.

But thank the Lord who saved thee, sir,
From passing through death's door."
"Canst thou not see? No joy for me
Remains in this world o'er.

For I still dream of her sweet face,
And think of her sweet song.
I'd rather I had followed her
Than that my life be long.

I see her in the sky above
With diamonds in her hair.
'Tis like a broken bone to know
I cannot join her there.

This tale is all I have of her;
I tell it but to praise
The many-colored bits of glass
That sparkled in her gaze."

The Mariner, whose hair is long,
Who feels he needs a snack,
Is gone, although the Wedding-Guest
Attempts to call him back.

He shakes his head like one amazed,
Who knows not what he knows,
And, with a halting step, back home
To Liverpool he goes.

I WILL ALARM ISLAMIC OWLS
WILLIAM CARLOS WILLIAMS

I will be alarming
the Islamic owls
that are in
the barn

and which
you warned me
are very jittery
and susceptible to loud noises

Forgive me
they see so well in the dark
so feathery
and so dedicated to Allah

IRS laW cOde
Oscar Wilde

Dramatis Personae:
SADLER HIGGINBOTHAM, *an auditor*
   for the Internal Revenue Service
AMBROSE PECK, *a taxpayer*

SADLER *(handing his card to Ambrose)* Good afternoon to you, sir.

AMBROSE And to you.

SADLER I trust you know the reason for this visit.

AMBROSE I do indeed. May I offer you some refreshment?

SADLER That is most generous of you.

AMBROSE It is easy to be generous when one is already expecting to lose a great deal of money. Your tea.

SADLER Thank you. But you needn't be as pessimistic as that. I am merely here to clarify a few minor tax matters which occasioned question.

AMBROSE It has been my experience that clarification never works in my favor. Why is it, for example, that whenever one has finally found an agreeable female dinner companion, invariably one is asked to clarify one's feelings about her? It makes a simple relationship so dreadfully awkward.

SADLER I'm afraid such questions are out of my purview. But shall we begin?

AMBROSE I regretfully expect we shall.

SADLER You've taken rather a lot of deductions here.

AMBROSE I can explain every last one.

SADLER I'm sure you can, and more's the pity. There's nothing quite so suspicious as having an explanation for something.

AMBROSE Well, if you would rather not hear them, I am only too happy not to provide them.

SADLER No, no. It is my burden and I must bear up under it. Now then—these travel expenses.

AMBROSE Oh, those are quite fraudulent.

SADLER You surprise me, sir. I thought you had explanations for all these items?

AMBROSE I do. But not all of them are true.

SADLER Your honesty does you credit.

AMBROSE The travel expenses in particular are one of my most extravagant concoctions. You will find that I have claimed business trips to several cities which do not, in point of fact, exist.

SADLER Really? I confess my expertise in geography is lacking.

AMBROSE That is only polite. For a man to excel in both mathematics and geography is quite intolerable. It bespeaks a promiscuous nature.

SADLER How true. Well, it is of no consequence if the cities are fictional. The Internal Revenue Service is not in the business of mapmaking. All that concerns me is whether the trips were business-related.

AMBROSE I can honestly say that I did nothing on any of those trips that was not business.

SADLER Very conscientious of you. Are any of the other deductions false?

AMBROSE It seems as if some of them must be, but my faculty for invention is really quite remarkable. Whatever entries may be false, even I can no longer discern which they are.

SADLER In that case, let us leave the deductions for a moment.

AMBROSE Leave them as long as you please.

SADLER I gather that you are a bachelor.

AMBROSE I do not deny the fact.

SADLER How is it, then, that you come by so many dependents?

AMBROSE My dear fellow, I do not come by them. They come by me. Or, more accurately, my house. They generally appear just before teatime, the scavengers, and invite themselves to stay. Alternatively, they will lurk on the pavement and pounce just as I attempt to board my carriage for dinner. Before I know it, I'm standing them three courses and drinks.

SADLER I well know the type. Sadly, such people—as trying as they are—do not fit the legal definition of a dependent.

AMBROSE How nettlesome!

SADLER It pains me deeply to be the bearer of such news.

AMBROSE Is there no remedy you can suggest?

SADLER Well—of course it will make no difference on last year's return, but—you might consider adopting the acquaintances in question.

AMBROSE Adopt those parasites! I had rather adopt a wood tick.

SADLER Merely a suggestion.

AMBROSE Although, were I to adopt them, all my good old friends would suddenly be my good-for-nothing wards. I mean to say, only a cad turns away a friend in need, but fathers are always giving their sons stern speeches about standing on their own two feet. You may have something there after all.

SADLER It gratifies me to hear it. Sadly, the deductions must still be removed.

AMBROSE Not to worry. Once I have cut off my impecunious relations-to-be, the money I shall save on dinners should more than make up the difference. Shall I expect a bill by the morning post?

SADLER You overestimate our efficiency considerably. Besides, given that we shall be charging you interest for your underpayment, it hardly behooves us to bill you promptly.

AMBROSE Indeed. Compound it how you will; I consider it a gratuity for advice well given.

SADLER *(collecting his hat and coat)* Should you find yourself in any similar predicaments, do not hesitate to call on me. My experience in the field is great. I have found, for instance, that hiring a troublesome friend as an employee is a sound method of ensuring that one never sees that person again, and offers several tax benefits as well.

AMBROSE How fascinating! I feel certain we shall find occasion to speak again soon. It has been a great pleasure.

SADLER I wholeheartedly concur.

AMBROSE Good afternoon to you.

SADLER And congratulations to you.

AMBROSE Congratulations?

SADLER On becoming a father, of course. *(They laugh.)* Good afternoon.

(Ambrose shuts the door behind Sadler.)

AMBROSE I now realise the importance of declaring earnings!

LIKABLE WILMA
WILLIAM BLAKE

Wilma, Wilma, in thy blouse,
Red-haired prehistoric spouse,
What immortal animator
Was thy slender waist's creator?

When the Rubble clan moved in,
Was Betty jealous of thy skin,
Thy noble nose, thy dimpled knee?
Did he who penciled Fred draw thee?

Wilma, Wilma, burning bright, ye
Cartoon goddess Aphrodite,
Was it Hanna or Barbera
Made thee hot as some caldera?

BASHŌ

(Two Haiku)

HAS B.O.

Swamp mist, eyes water—
Why is that monk still wearing
Winter robes in June?

AH, SOB

A yellow snake eats
The robin's lone precious egg—
You motherfucker

HEN GONADS
OGDEN NASH

I thought running a chicken breeding farm would be a simple
 matter,
Just pipe some romantic music into the chicken coop and
 wait for the proverbial little feet's pitter-patter,
But it's turned out to be trickier than that to affect a chicken's
 libido,
Because I just don't know what chickens find attractive,
 I mean, when I go out on the town I dress to the nines,
 but does a chicken prefer a rooster in an opera hat and
 tuxedo?
Well, I can say definitively that she does not,
And if anyone has been considering the purchase of a
 rooster-sized tuxedo and opera hat you should come
 down here and take a look at this reasonably priced
 used set I've got.
Neither did my backup plan of spiking the chicken feed with
 Spanish fly produce results,
Nor the screening of nature documentaries intended for
 adults,
Nor threats of arroz con pollo,

Nor … well, I don't want to give all the embarrassing details,
    but let's just say there's nothing quite like asking a
    salesman if he has a vibrator specifically designed to
    stimulate hen gonads to make one feel like a total yo-yo.
Yes, I'm distinctly subpar at stirring romantic longings in
    the loins of a chicken, and when it comes to setting
    up blind dates in the poultry world, I make a pretty
    poor yenta,
So as for breeding chickens, perhaps I wasn't menta.

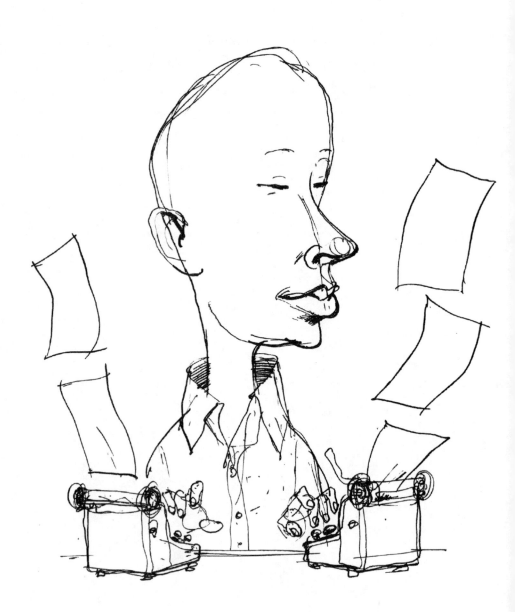

niCe smug me
e.e. cummings

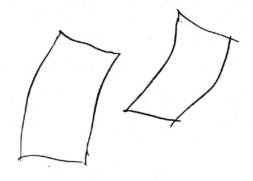

this here verse's
disjunct
    i used to
    stick to regular metered
            poetry
now i write onetwothreefourfive poemsjustlikethat
                Jesus

but this is simple work
         and what i want to know is
how much am i going to get paid for this
mister editor

At this point in his career, cummings was so cocky that, for the next five years, he used the same title for all his poems. This made things significantly simpler for the many critics who derided his work, as they only had to write one bad review each and reprint it every time cummings published a new poem.

nice smug me
e.e. cummings

nice smug me lived in a pretty hip town
(with up so noses snobs looking down)
saks moomba vong prada
i wore my mesclun i ate my uggs

Women and men(both wealthy and rich)
opened their mouths to gossip and bitch
as many by many we spent our bucks
scarf tie hat tux

noon by drunk and cab by home
we laughed our loves and felled our rome
(gin vodka wine vermouth)i
said my shouldnts i scorned my shoulds

Women and men(both thin and tall)
glamour vogue esquire elle
smiled my jokes and slept my myth
cindy adams liz smith

HORRID PLANET
HAROLD PINTER

Dramatis Personae:
C-3P0, *an android*
R2-D2, *an android*
a group of **JAWAS**

(A spaceship rescue pod crashes to the surface of a desert. Two robots emerge.)

C-3P0 Well.

(Long pause.)

C-3P0 There's a lot of sand here, that's all I have to say. *(Pause.)* A lot of sand. *(Pause.)* Don't care for it. No. Don't care for it at all. *(Pause.)* And too much sun. *(Pause.)* I don't mind a bit of sun, of course. I can't think of anyone who minds a bit of sun. It's nice. Warms you up. Glints off you, it's cheerful. But there's a limit. And then there's all this sand. *(Pause.)* Too much sand. It's interesting. When you think about it. Eh? What you do, when you're crash-landing on a planet, you're worried about landing in the sea. The sea! Because you'd be stranded, wouldn't you. No land in sight. And then you crash. And this is what you get. Sand. *(Pause.)* It's funny, when you think about it.

(Pause.)

R2-D2 *(Beeps ominously.)*

C-3P0 What are you trying to say? Eh?

R2-D2 *(Beeps ambiguously.)*

C-3P0 What exactly are you getting at?

R2-D2 *(Beeps angrily.)*

C-3P0 You're saying it's all my fault.

R2-D2 *(Beeps noncommittally.)*

C-3P0 Don't you try to accuse me. I didn't ask to come here. Get sand in my joints. Overheat in the sun. Oh yes. You think you can look at me with that red light, and I'll come apart like a Christmas cracker. You with your message from the Princess. You're nothing but a glorified tape recorder, that's what you are. I'm stronger than you think. I'm watching you. I've got your number, I have. I've got your number to one million decimal places. It's just . . . I'm . . . all I need . . . if I could just . . . for a bit . . . so hot . . .

R2-D2 *(Beeps mockingly.)*

C-3P0 *(falling to the ground)* You think you've beaten me, don't you? Eh? I'll show you yet. Just you wait. Your time will come.

R2-D2 *(Beeps victoriously.)*

C-3P0 I'll get you yet. You'll see.

(Pause.)

(A group of Jawas appears and captures the droids, carrying them away to a droid storage unit.)

R2-D2 *(Beeps fretfully.)*

C-3P0 You see? Eh? I warned you. That's what a bad attitude gets you. Not me. I look on the sunny side. Not that it does me any good. Not with you. I got you dragging me down. But that'll show you. Try to accuse me of . . . what did I ever do? I look out for you, I take care of you, don't I? And you repay me with bile. I'd like to see you try to escape from Imperial battle droids by yourself, mate, that's what I'd like to see. Now that would be comical. But here you are. We're in the same boat now, aren't we? Lot of good being all high and mighty does you now. Oh yes. Now you see. I told you I'd show you, didn't I? And I have, I've beaten you. That's right, my lad. You're nicked. Might as well just pack it in. I've won.

(A Jawa removes C-3P0's head.)

R2-D2 *(Beeps grief-strickenly.)*

(Blackout. All we can see is R2-D2's red light, staring forlornly at the audience. Soon that fades out as well.)

bAngles linGer

Allen Ginsberg

I.

I saw the worst bands of my generation outselling Madness, boring
      ridiculous catchy,
dragging themselves through the three-chord charts each night looking for
      a leggy hit,
muttonheaded singers walking like the ancient Egyptians unconcerned
      about finding intellect in the gray matter of fans,
who radios and Walkmans and ringing-eared and high stayed up dancing
      in the supernatural darkness of hand-stamping clubs surfing
      across the heads of mosh pits contemplating grunge,
who blared their songs by Heaven 17 and saw MTV veejays staggering on
      camera while intoxicated,
who were expelled from the record stores for rowdy & shoplifting obscure
      tapes down the pockets of their pants,
who skanked all night to the English Beat as Bangles singles sold like
      husbands to Zsa Zsa and punks absorbed their Fugazi, listening
      to the crash of drums on the hideous jukebox,
who scored autographs from rockstars rockstars rockstars breathing in their
      blow toward talkative charm in narcissist night,

who climbed up America's Top Forty this actually happened and walked
away unknown and forgotten into the ghastly haze of second-rate
state fair tours & shopping malls, not even one bowl of green
M&M's,
with the one hit that made them a wonder for life belching out of their
cheap rented amps to hear a thousand times.

II.

What finks of beatbox and programming bashed open their skulls and ate
up their taste and imagination?
Moloko! Soul II Soul! Filter! Underworld! Rare tracks and unobtainable
b-sides! Roadies streaming out of the tour bus! Boys dubbing on
mix boards! Old men signing up *NSYNC!
Moloko! Moloko! Nightmare of Moloko! Moloko the mindless! Techno
Moloko! Moloko the wearer of tight sweaters!
Moloko whose drummer is pure machinery! Moloko whose songs are disco
fodder! Moloko whose name is silly! Moloko whose producer is
the singer's boyfriend! Moloko who is not a doctor!
Moloko! Moloko! Robot accompanists! *Batman & Robin* soundtracks!
skeletal remixes! bland choruses! other unpleasant things!

Moloko! Moloko! Did I mention Moloko? Moloko! Molokomolokomoloko!
They broke their backs lifting Moloko to playlists! lifting the shitty to radio
      which emits waves flying everywhere around us!
Lame oldies playing in a diner! They hear it all! the mild whines! the hollow
       yelps! They sing along! They know all the words! to China Grove!
       Beat It! La Isla Bonita! Down with the radio! into the trash!

III.

R.E.M.! I'm with you in Rockville
     where they're cooler than I am
I'm with you in Rockville
     where you must sell many disks
I'm with you in Rockville
     where you imitate the sound of Roger McGuinn
I'm with you in Rockville
     where your condition has become famous and is reported on the
     radio
I'm with you in Rockville
     where fifty million dollars will never return Bill Berry to his drums
     again from his pilgrimage to live on a farm

I'm with you in Rockville

> where there are twenty-five-billion Gen-Xers still unable to forget
> the chorus of "Manic Monday"

I'm with you in Rockville

> where we wake up horrified out of our REM sleep by our own
> clock radios braying wretched Steve Winwood he's come to play
> indelible cliches the clock face illuminates itself fists pound snooze
> buttons O luckless listeners run outside O sleepy screaming fans of
> alt-rock the eternal war is here O victory forget your earplugs we're
> free

I'm with you in Rockville

> in my dreams you play "Driver 8" all evening on the radios across
> America instead of that Cranberries song I hear every damn night

IS A SPERM LIKE A WHALE?
WILLIAM SHAKESPEARE

Shall I compare thee to a sperm whale, sperm?
Thou art more tiny and more resolute:
Rough tides may sway a sea-bound endotherm,
But naught diverts thy uterine commute.
Sometime too fierce the eye of squid may glint
And make a stout cetacean hunter quail;
Methinks 'twould take much more than bilious squint
To shake thee off the cunning ovum's trail.
Yet still thou art not so unlike, thou two,
Both coursing through a dark uncharted brine
While fore and aft there swims thy fellow crew;
And note this echo, little gamete mine:
As whales spray salty water from their spout,
So with a salty spray dost thou come out.

I'M LEERY, JOCK
JOYCE KILMER

I doubt that I shall ever view
Another football game with you.
You holler nonstop in my ear,
For every tackle makes you cheer,
Or bellow in a wounded way,
Depending on who makes the play.
I do not understand the charm
Of watching athletes doing harm.
Football's played for fools like you,
But I have better things to do.

ELLEN'S SIAMESE TWIN
TENNESSEE WILLIAMS

Dramatis Personae:

ELLEN, *a vivacious young Southern girl*

LAURA, *her shy Siamese twin*

TOM, *their brother*

JIM, *a gentleman caller*

ELLEN Tom! Oh, Tom!

TOM Yes, Ellen?

ELLEN Is it true? Is your friend coming to dinner tonight?

TOM Well, yes, Ellen, but—

ELLEN Oh, this is wonderful, just wonderful! Laura, isn't it wonderful?

LAURA You asked a…a man…to dinner? Here? But, Ellen, when did you—I don't *remember*…

ELLEN You were *asleep*, Laura. Sleeping, sleeping, always sleeping. It's just lucky for you that I don't mind sitting and reading! It's an opportunity to *better* myself. You should do the same, you know. A woman should be able to converse on any topic—if she's interested in finding a husband, that is!

TOM I wouldn't get your hopes up, Ellen. He's just a fellow from work. Don't start making plans.

ELLEN I don't know what you're talking about, Tom Wingfield.

TOM Of course not.

LAURA Do we even know this boy, Ellen?

ELLEN He's not a boy, Laura. He's a *man*.

TOM Oh, my God!

ELLEN Well, what would *you* call him then, Tom? Honestly!

TOM Look, all I'm saying is don't make this a bigger deal than it is. I didn't tell him it was…that you'd *nagged* me into it! I just invited him over for dinner. Now, if he likes you, well, that's fine. But just don't get *ahead* of yourself.

ELLEN Well, of course not, Tom! The idea!

LAURA You didn't answer my—*question*—

ELLEN Oh, I don't know who he is, Laura! Someone we went to high school with, I think. John or Jim or something.

TOM Jim.

LAURA Not—Jim O'Connor?

TOM Yeah. Did you know him?

LAURA Yes! That is—he didn't know *me*. We talked, once or twice. But I—oh, Ellen, I can't, I can't possibly have dinner with him!

ELLEN Don't be ridiculous, Laura. I doubt he'll even take any notice of you. *(The doorbell rings.)* There he is now. *(She walks toward the door but Laura struggles against her.)*

LAURA Ellen—*please!*

ELLEN *(melodically, to the door)* Just a moment!

LAURA *(whispering passionately)* I can't!

ELLEN Laura, let go of the divan so I can answer the door. *(Laura, close to tears, shakes her head and clutches the divan tighter.)*

TOM Oh, for ... I'll get it.

(Ellen pushes Laura down onto the divan and sits beside her as Tom opens the door. Ellen has unintentionally sat between Laura and the doorway, blocking her from view.)

JIM Hi, Tom! Oh—I didn't know you had a sister. You been holding out on me?

TOM Two sisters.

JIM Huh? *(Laura peeks out, nervously.)* Oh—hello! Didn't see you there! Well, pleased to meet you both. Jim. Jim O'Connor.

ELLEN *(pointedly)* Tom, hadn't you better check on dinner?

TOM I guess I'd better. *(He exits.)*

ELLEN Have a seat, Mr. O'Connor!

JIM Call me Jim. Say, you look awful familiar. It's not ... Ellen, is it? Weren't we in high school together?

ELLEN *(delighted to be remembered)* Why, I believe we were!

JIM Sure! I think we even sat together in geometry!

ELLEN My goodness—what a coincidence!

JIM *(to Laura)* And what's *your* name?

(Laura is too petrified to answer.)

ELLEN *(irritated, but pretending to be unruffled)* This is my Siamese twin, Laura.

JIM I never knew you had a Siamese twin, Ellen!

ELLEN No?

JIM You certainly never said anything about it in school.

ELLEN Well, I just—never thought to mention it!

JIM I had no idea. A Siamese twin. That's something! Well, hello, Laura!

LAURA Hello.

JIM Laura. That's a nice name. Not very Siamese, though!

LAURA Oh! Well … of course … I mean …

JIM *(laughing)* I'm just joshing.

(As the laughter subsides, there is an awkward pause.)

LAURA I—don't suppose you remember me.

JIM Well, I thought you looked a little familiar, too, but I wasn't sure … but … of course—I remember you now! You were that quiet girl who was always attached to Ellen!

LAURA *(shyly)* Yes.

JIM Well, isn't that something. And here I find out the two of you are Siamese twins.

ELLEN It's a small world, it certainly is! Enough about us, though, Jim. Why don't you tell us about yourself? I'm sure you've got simply *lots* of exciting plans for the future. Why—

JIM *(ignoring her)* It's just that the two of you just seemed so different, I never would have guessed you were related, let alone *twins!* I mean, you seemed so shy, and—well, *sad*, Laura! I would have thought, with a sister like Ellen—

ELLEN *(flirtatiously)* It's true, I was always very popular. I'm so glad you noticed, Jim.

LAURA *(with a nervous glance at Ellen)* Oh, well—my sister is wonderful, of course, but ... she always walked so much faster than me, I was always *stumbling*. It made me feel so ... awkward and— conspicuous!

JIM I never noticed that. I mean—you always looked okay to me.

LAURA Oh ... I ...

ELLEN *(attempting to regain Jim's attention)* Jim, you're making her nervous. Laura doesn't like to talk about herself. Now—

JIM *(rising)* Well, that's just a lack of self-confidence, is what that is! Gosh! Why—I bet you've never even danced with someone!

LAURA No—of course not!

JIM Would you like to?

LAURA Oh, I—I don't—

ELLEN I'll dance with you, Jim. Just follow me, Laura, I'm sure you'll do fine.

JIM You know how to dance?

ELLEN I admit my dancing experience has been limited to watching other girls, but I believe I can manage! A positive attitude can accomplish anything, that's what I say!

JIM I agree! We'll need some music, though.

LAURA I'll wind—the *Victrola* . . . *(She and Ellen rise so that Laura can reach the Victrola. A waltz is heard.)*

JIM Perfect! *(He takes Ellen's right hand and begins to lead her in a waltz. Laura awkwardly tries to follow but cannot keep up and keeps bumping into Ellen.)* Here, Laura, it's easier than you think. Look—*(He switches from Ellen to Laura so he can lead her more clearly. Laura seems a bit more confident.)*

LAURA Oh!

JIM See, it's not so hard! *(Ellen, jealous of the attention, trips Laura. The three fall into an ungainly heap.)*

ELLEN I'm so sorry . . . I lost my balance!

JIM Are you all right, Laura?

LAURA *(crying)* You horrible . . . *jealous*—

JIM *(rising)* Laura, Ellen . . . look, I don't know what you think, but you've got the wrong idea. There's no point fighting over me.

LAURA You're not . . . already seeing someone, are you?

JIM No, but . . . I like you *both*. If you see what I mean.

LAURA *(shocked)* Oh!

ELLEN Oh, Laura, don't be so old-fashioned. *(Calling)* Is that dinner ready, Tom?

TOM *(entering)* Has been for a while.

ELLEN Well, why ever didn't you tell us? Let's eat! *(She exits, Laura in tow, glancing shyly at Jim, who follows, winking at Tom as he goes.)*

TOM I was glad it seemed like there might finally be someone to take care of my sisters, because I had to escape. I couldn't take it any more—working at the factory, coming home and listening to Ellen talk all night long. I had already signed up with a traveling sideshow. I was going to be the man in the gorilla costume. You know the act —you walk into this tent, and there's a girl in a cage. Next thing you know, she turns into a gorilla and breaks down the door of the cage, and everyone runs out, screaming. That was always a beautiful moment, chasing them out of the tent. Looking back on it, I don't know if it was the best job I could have chosen. It seemed like every one of the freaks in the sideshow reminded me of Laura and Ellen, reminded me of the responsibilities I'd left behind. I hope things worked out all right for them. *(He exits.)*

ELLEN *(heard from the other room, amid the clinking of tableware)* Jim, you *are* a card! I think you just might be one of us! You hear? *One ... of ... us!*

(Laughter. Blackout.)

AN E-MAIL
A. A. MILNE

Whatever I do, there's always Pooh,
There's always Pooh and Me.
"Let's write an e-mail," I say to Pooh.
"That sounds like a wonderful thing to do,"
He says. I say, "I think so too."
"Let's write it together," says Pooh, says he.
"Let's write it together," says Pooh.

"Where is the caps lock?" I said to Pooh.
("Caps what?" said Pooh to me.)
"I think I'd rather if everyone knew
How excited I am." "Of course," said Pooh.
So I typed a whole screen, but I wasn't through.
"I think it needs more," said Pooh, said he.
"I think it needs more," said Pooh.

"Let's add some JPEGs," I said to Pooh.
"Yes, let's," said Pooh to me.
I searched online and found a few,
And I showed them one by one to Pooh.
"They're pretty big. Do you think they'll do?"
"I think they'll do," said Pooh, said he.
"I think they'll do," said Pooh.

"Where shall we send it?" I said to Pooh.
"I don't know," said Pooh to me.
"I know who I shall send it to!
All of my friends—three hundred and two!"
"They'll all want to read it, I'm sure," said Pooh.
"I certainly would," said Pooh, said he,
"I *love* to get e-mails from you."

So whatever I do, there's always Pooh,
There's always Pooh and Me.
"Thank goodness for you," I said to Pooh,
And Pooh agreed, "It's certainly true
That two are better for thinking things through."
"I'm not sure that got sent," says Pooh, says he.
"Better send it again," says Pooh.

ERROL FLYNN'S NOT DEAD
ALFRED LORD TENNYSON

He grabs the rope with withered hands,
Swings through the air and softly lands;
Girt with a silver sword he stands.

That rotting man is Errol Flynn;
He bares a grey and toothless grin,
And like a zombie eats my skin.

KONG RAN MY DEALERSHIP
GERARD MANLEY HOPKINS

TO OUR SALES LEADER

I hired last summer someone simian, King
    Kong of Indies islands, fifty-foot-fierce Gorilla, out of hiding
    After falling, feigning final death but breathing yet, and biding
Time there, how he swore that he could sell any third-rate thing
In a car lot! To the old, old Ford with a ding,
    As a snake oil sales spiel hooks a hill-hick, the ape was guiding
    A mark by monstrous hand, the rube then riding
Afar in that car,—to escape him, an appeasement on the wing!

Brute blarney to offer as options wheels, brakes, boot, seat
    Buckles, AND to roar. He breaks from his pen, he lumbers
Towards pale patrons, so dangerous, O who will he eat?

    No wonder of it: sheer fear makes Kong's sales numbers
Rise, though swift syringe stuck in his feet
    Can tranquilize, so King Kong slumbers.

Edward Fitzgerald's first translations of Omar Khayyam retained much of Khayyam's original, although in later versions the yak became sheep, and Omar was presented as a more feminine figure who wore a bonnet and skirt, and carried one of those crooked sticks. While a simplified version of that translation gained popularity as a nursery rhyme, the first translation is considered the definitive one and is presented here.

AH, MY YAK ROAM
OMAR KHAYYAM

I

Behold! I tend a Herd of woolly Yak
That wander o'er the Hills in one great Pack:
    But Lo! the Yak have vanished in the Night,
And God alone knows if they shall come back.

II

Dreaming on the Hillside where I lay
I heard a soothing Voice within me say
    "Fear not, my Child, if you will leave them be,
The Dawn will bring them as it brings the Day."

III

And, as the Cock crew, Light did reach my Eyes
And silhouette my Yak against the Skies.
    They lumbered down to meet me at the Lake,
Their Tails behind them, swishing at the Flies.

SKINNY DOMICILE
EMILY DICKINSON

I have a skinny Domicile—
Its Door is very narrow.
'Twill keep—I hope—the Reaper out—
His Scythe—and Bones—and Marrow.

Since Death is not a portly Chap,
The Entrance must be thin—
So—when my Final Moment comes—
He cannot wriggle in.

That's why I don't go out that much—
I can't fit through that Portal.
How dumb—to waste my Social Life
On Plans to be—immortal—

I rEuse dip
Euripides

Dramatis Personae:
GEORGE COSTANZA, *an insensitive man*
BETSY, *a woman George is dating*
DR. ALLENWOOD, *Betsy's family doctor*
TIMMY, *Betsy's brother*
CHORUS, *a group of judgmental New Yorkers*

GEORGE
O, how I wish the woman whom I date,
Betsy, touched by Aphrodite's hand,
Were having sex with me. You gods, hear me!
My overtures are ever misconstrued,
Or some external force doth interrupt.
Behold, how dreaded Thanatos did touch
My out-of-reach beloved's agèd aunt,
Just at the moment I was closing in.
Now, yet untasting of her sweetest pleasure,
I am called to join her in Detroit,
The place her aunt will start the lonely trek
To Hades' realm. O bitter circumstance!
I am no wealthy man, and this is dear,
To reach a distant city at such speed.

CHORUS LEADER

Your fortunes fare much better than you think.
To hold her hand in solemn consolation
Can only draw the two of you together.
Go, throw yourself upon the mercy
Of the airline. Claim her aunt is yours,
And they may pity you, for grieving's sake.
Be warned! They may demand a token of thee,
Proof this death is no invention. Take care!

GEORGE

I shall. Your words give me great comfort!
Betsy, I come, a hellhound could not stop me!

(He exits.)

CHORUS *(chanting)*

Zeus speed you on your way, George Costanza!
And yet we fear your inexperience:
Let not your pride destroy you, now you've come
So far to join your Betsy, here in Detroit.

(Betsy and George enter.)

BETSY

I praise the gods you've come, my darling.

GEORGE

It is a lover's duty, but no burden.
I am your lover, am I not?

BETSY

Of course.

GEORGE

The wake is well appointed. Will you eat?
I saw some olives that I long to taste.

BETSY

My tears have fed me enough. Go on ahead.

(She exits.)

CHORUS

George, do not forget your purpose;
The proof of death is yet to be obtained!
The family doctor stands now at the table,
Near the bowl of hummus. Do not flinch!

(Enter Dr. Allenwood)

GEORGE

Are you the doctor who performed the rite?

DR. ALLENWOOD

I serve the family in death and life.

GEORGE

So dear to Betsy was her aunt, I beg
A favor. She desires some memento,
The better to recall this loss. Perhaps
A certificate of death, to grace her wall.

DR. ALLENWOOD

A noble thought. I'll write it and return.

(He exits.)

CHORUS

All is accomplished! George may now relax;
He tastes a bite of hummus on a pita.
But when our guard is down, the danger's worst.
George Costanza, now you stand in peril.

(Enter Timmy.)

TIMMY

I saw you place your pita in that dip
Once, and then again. You bit the pita,
Yet you dipped it. What could drive a man
To such a vile thing? I feel defiled.
It's like you licked the hummus with your tongue.
I beg you, dip just once, and then move on.

GEORGE

That is not my custom.

TIMMY

You defy me?

GEORGE

Why should I change the way I eat for you?
Watch me as I dip a third time. Ha!

TIMMY

Accursèd man! I banish thee forever!
Our lands are poison to you, and what's more,
If you touch my sister, Betsy, you will die.
I'll see to it myself, I swear. Now go!
I would not test my patience, little man.

(George exits hastily. Timmy follows.)

CHORUS

How quick our fate can change. Poor George Costanza!
No proof of death, his Betsy gone,
His pita left unfinished. All is lost.
It seems sometimes the joys of life
Are given only to then be snatched away,
Though, honestly, he was being an idiot.

YOGA AluMnae
Maya Angelou

A Lotus, A Cobra, A Downward-Facing Dog,
Names of positions long since mastered,
Marked on your exams.

You, created only a little saner than
The Moonies, have crouched eight weeks in
The candlelit classroom,
Have lain as long
Facedown in extreme pain,
Your mouths spilling chants
Learned phonetically.

The Instructor cries out today,
you may stand on your head,
But do not hurt your neck.

Each of you a spacy hippie,
Delicate and spookily thin,
From eating nothing but miso soup.
Yes, today I call you to your classrooms,
And you will study yoga no more. Come,

Clad in leotards and I will play the music
The CD Store Guy gave to me when I asked if
He had any John Tesh.

So teach the Yuppie, the Muscle Boy, the Geek,
The Working Mom and the Scary Punk Squatter, the Clique,
The Wannabe, the Hipster, the Star, the Snob,
The Pickup Artist, the Model, the Slob.
They stretch. They all stretch
The muscles of the Soul.

Come to me, here beside the Exercise Mat.
Plant your shoes in a locker, sit beside the Exercise Mat.

Each of you, graduate of some passed
Two-month course, has been paid for.

Here on the pulse of this new day
May you have the grace under pressure to look
Straight into your student's eyes, into

Your pupil's face, your acolyte

And say simply

Very simply

With hope—

I'm sorry you threw your back out, please for the love of
God don't sue me.

CARRY HUGE COFFEE
GEOFFREY CHAUCER

In tholde dayes of the towne Seatel,
Of whos charmes Nirvana fans yet pratel,
Al that reyny land fayn slepen late.
Thus ofte a sutor failled to keepe a date;
And werkers reched offices at noon,
Noddyng of although the sunne shoon;
Husbondes were too tyred by the eve
A staf for plesyng wyves to acheve.

    Now to this citie in a languor stukke,
Came a fair knyght cleped Sterrebukke,
Beryng benes from a forein land
Ygrounde to a poudre in his hand,
From which a potent brew could he deryve
That causeth wery peple to revyve.
Whan word aboute his draghte hadde sprede,
To his shoppe the custumers al spedde
Til everich veine felte a rush of blood,
With humours boyed upward by that flood.
Soone men who herd the crowyng cok
Wolde rise withoute cursyng at the clok,

The thoughte of facyng daylight not so bleke
With coffey bryngyng roses to the cheke
And helpyng them to holde their swords alofte
And shethe them before they falle softe.
　　Sterrebukke so bygan to thynke
Of other ways to selle the same drynke.
With stemed milk and sprenkled cynamone,
'Twas fit, he sayde, for kynges on the throne;
The capuchino joyned thus his wares,
As wel as mocas, sweter than eclares,
And lattes riche in creme, ofte fresen
And beten to a froth in sumer seson,
And tall espressos armured with cappes
To stoppen scaldyng spilles into lappes
As may hap when one is in a hurry
Upon a pilgrymage to Caunterbury.

DREARY HOT PORK
DOROTHY PARKER

Bacon is fatty;
Ham's sickly sweet;
Just one sausage patty
Will widen your seat.

A plateful of wurst?
Your thighs will soon chafe.
More chops? No, I'll burst.
What a pain to keep *treyf.*

A wEe bladder
Edward Albee

Dramatis Personae:
GEORGE, *a middle-aged college professor*
MARTHA, *his wife*
NICK, *a younger professor*
HONEY, *his wife*

(Lights come up on a tense scene in a suburban living room. George stands at the entrance to the kitchen thuggishly clutching a gin bottle by the neck. Martha is on the floor in front of the couch. Honey is shrinking into an armchair; Nick sits on the arm protectively.)

GEORGE *(quietly)* All right, Martha. If you want to lose yourself in a bottle, I'm not going to stop you. But I'm not going to help you either. You're going to have to come and get the bottle yourself. *(He dangles it tantalizingly.)* Icky wittle bottle for Martha.

NICK That's not necessary.

GEORGE Not necessary? *(He chuckles to himself.)* I! I SHALL DECIDE WHAT IS NECESSARY!

MARTHA *(struggling to her feet)* That's a laugh. When have you ever decided anything?

GEORGE We shall see, won't we?

MARTHA All right, buster. If that's how you want to play it ... *(She walks unsteadily towards him, then stops.)* Hang on, I'll be right back.

(She quickly stumbles through the hallway door. There is an awkward pause.)

GEORGE Hm. *(Not sure what to do with the bottle, he puts it down on a nearby table.)*

HONEY Has the yelling stopped? My head is all poundy.

GEORGE Well...for the moment, so it seems.

NICK You shouldn't drink so much brandy, honey.

HONEY I guess not. Do you have any aspirin?

GEORGE Well, probably, but... *(We hear the sound of a flushing toilet from offstage. Martha soon reenters.)* Ah! The prodigal returneth!

MARTHA *(scornfully, with a wave)* YAAAH! *(She makes a beeline for the gin bottle, which George has momentarily forgotten. She grabs it before he can react.)*

NICK Looks like she got you.

GEORGE Sadly, yes. I am got and will never, ever be ungot, try how I may.

MARTHA *(mock sympathy)* Aw! *(She pours herself a generous glass of gin.)*

GEORGE When Martha *gets* someone, they stay got.

MARTHA That's right, baby. *(She takes a big swig.)*

GEORGE You think you're so smart, don't you, Martha. Humiliating me in front of everyone. But if I'm stuck with you, you're stuck with me. Like a dog with its teeth in your ankle. Oh, yes, I have teeth, Martha. *(He advances on her.)* HOW DO YOU LIKE THAT?

NICK *(rising)* Don't get violent, now, or—

GEORGE Or what? What'll you do, eh, sonny boy?

NICK You'll find out.

GEORGE Will I. Here's your champion, Martha! Your knight in shining armor.

MARTHA *(vaguely)* Uh-huh. Oh dear. Excuse me for just a second. *(She runs out again.)*

HONEY *(calling after her)* Could you get me some aspirin while you're in there?

GEORGE Oh, for the love of…

NICK *(off balance)* Well … all right then. *(He sits down on the couch as if he has made his point. There is a pause.)*

HONEY Is she throwing up?

GEORGE No. Martha doesn't … throw up. She has enough poison in her bloodstream already that she's immune. But Martha … the thing about Martha is … she has a … small bladder, you know. She doesn't like to talk about it.

HONEY That's terrible.

GEORGE Yes, it is quite a burden. For people who drink as much as we do. But we go on.

HONEY You drink anyway!

GEORGE We do.

HONEY It's courageous is what it is.

(Another flush. Martha returns.)

MARTHA Here's your aspirin. *(She throws the aspirin bottle to Honey, who catches it.)*

HONEY Whee!

MARTHA Where were we?

GEORGE I've lost track.

NICK Well, it doesn't matter, she'll be running out the door again soon enough.

(Silence.)

MARTHA You told them.

GEORGE It may have slipped out...

MARTHA YOU TOLD THEM!

HONEY Well, it wasn't that much of a secret. *(She giggles.)* It's not like we couldn't see you leave the room.

MARTHA I WAS VERY CASUAL ABOUT THAT!

NICK But...you *left the room*. And then the toilet flushed. And you came back.

MARTHA *(turning on George)* This is your fault. Daddy warned me about you. He said I'd never be able to trust you and he was right.

GEORGE Peck, peck, peck. I warned you not to fool with me. Go on. Peck, peck, peck.

MARTHA I'll peck if I want. He said...excuse me, I have to go...put this bottle of aspirin back in the medicine cabinet before it gets lost. *(She takes the bottle and exits.)*

GEORGE Oh, it's pathetic.

NICK But why is she so embarrassed about it?

GEORGE *Martha*...in addition to having a small bladder...has a *shy* bladder. She cannot...*perform*...if she thinks people can hear her. It is...a deadly combination.

NICK Oh. *(They all listen for the flush. There is none. Eventually Martha storms back in.)*

MARTHA You bastard! What have you done to me?

GEORGE I haven't done anything. Now listen. I've reconsidered. Have another drink. *(He hands her the gin bottle.)* I'm glad to help.

MARTHA You ... *(She exits again.)*

HONEY Darling, I think I'd like to go home.

NICK Yeah, this whole evening has been sort of socially awkward. I'm surprised we stuck it out this long.

GEORGE All righty, kids. Go on home. Back to your little beds. *(They exit while he is talking. He carries on anyway.)* Read yourselves a story. "Once upon a time, there was a little boy. And he was kidnapped by a witch. And—" *(Martha reappears.)* No luck, dear?

MARTHA You know perfectly well.

GEORGE But the guests have gone. It's just the two of us now.

NANCY Just the two of us?

GEORGE Yes. It'll be better now. You'll see. I'll plug my ears.

MARTHA And hum?

GEORGE Of course.

MARTHA You shouldn't have told them, George.

GEORGE I know.

MARTHA *I* didn't tell them about the time bomb implanted in your brain.

GEORGE Well, they'll find out eventually.

(She exits. He explodes. We hear a flush.)

DH
H.D.

DH, rend open the ball,
rip apart the seams,
bash it to pieces.

Pitchers can't hit
in the AL—
you are better than the pitcher
that chokes up and bunts
and runs pell-mell
yet rounds no base.

Hit the ball—
plough through it,
cleave it with the Ginsu knife
of your bat.

brR, Footrest
Robert Frost

This ottoman is in my way.
I tripped on it again today;
It chills me with a nameless fear
To think it sees me as its prey.

My loving wife must think it queer
That I am always falling here
As I am walking past the chair.
How comical I must appear.

When I remember to beware
The wicked footrest lurking there,
I do not stumble in a sprawl,
And yet such instances are rare.

My house is cozy, warm, and small,
With just one thing that wrecks it all:
The ottoman that makes me fall,
The ottoman that makes me fall.

WANT WHAM! LIT
WALT WHITMAN

Out at the concert endlessly rocking,

Out at the festival show, the musical circus,

Out at the hour before midnight,

Over the darkened stage, and the wings beyond, where the
roadies, tripping on cords, scurry around, pot-headed,
punch-drunk,

Here come the light technicians,

Up from the pitch-black stage on ladders, climbing with
flashlights to peer among the wires.

In the dressing rooms of the stars that pace and fret,

In the dressing rooms of Wham!—by the electrical outage
subdued,

With candles hurriedly lit, flickering, and dripping wax
like tears,

With no beginning notes of "Careless Whisper," there on
the unlit stage,

With the thousands of fans on the grass, unwilling to
leave,

With a myriad of four-letter words,

With the word stronger and more offensive than any,

With such, like Job beset, a helpless anger,

Like Pharaoh, the plague of darkness overhead passing,

Destroying—and at the center, pompadour'd,

A man—yet by this tantrum just a boy again,

Telling his manager off, insisting on lights,

He, dreamboat of girls and boys, bandmate of Andrew
Ridgeley,

Waiting all night to headline—but swiftly thwarted by
surges,

George Michael is pissed.

mopTop darTS
Tom Stoppard

Dramatis Personae:
JOHN, *a Beatle*
PAUL, *a Beatle*
GEORGE, *a Beatle*
RINGO, *a Beatle*
RICHARD LESTER, *a film director*

(The Beatles are sitting in a bar, laughing and chatting up girls. John turns to Paul.)

JOHN *Darts.*
PAUL Do what, love?

(John jerks his head toward a dartboard on the wall of the bar.)

JOHN Come on then.
PAUL Oh, you go ahead.

(Paul turns back to the girl he was talking to. John grabs him by the collar and drags him past where George and Ringo are seated.)

GEORGE What's up with you two?

JOHN Same thing that'll be up with you and Ringo in a moment. We're playing darts.

RINGO You don't look like it.

JOHN Cheeky. Just for that, you can be my partner.

(Ringo rolls his eyes.)

GEORGE I don't really understand the appeal of darts.

JOHN It has a long and proud history, me lad, which you clearly do not appreciate.

GEORGE Clearly.

PAUL I don't trust a game that can't count to twenty.

JOHN *(incensed)* Now, there's a good reason for that.

PAUL Oh yes? And what's that?

JOHN Well, the numbering system of the ancient Celts was very different from the one we have today—

PAUL Come off it, you have absolutely no idea.

JOHN I have many ideas, but I make no claims upon their accuracy.

RINGO *(stepping up to the line)* It's really not so complicated. If a player is, for instance, shooting for a triple twenty—which is the highest scoring spot on the board, although most non-darts-playing individuals assume it is the bull's-eye—should the player miss, the numbers on either side of the twenty are both low numbers, thereby punishing the player for his bad aim. Hence the irregular numbering.

(Pause.)

PAUL Cor.

JOHN I always knew he had hidden depths.

RINGO Ssh.

(Ringo shoots a triple twenty. John cheers.)

PAUL *(turning to John, accusing)* You bloody cheat!

JOHN What?

PAUL Leave it to you to put the expert on your team!

JOHN I had no idea. *(He begins speaking in a high-pitched voice.)* I'm innocent, officer! It was me upbringing.

GEORGE Oi, Ringo. Where'd you learn to throw like that, then?

RINGO Well, it's all physics, isn't it? The application of simple laws, analysis of vectors …

GEORGE Yeah, but it's impossible to have full knowledge of all variables.

PAUL He's got you there, Ringo.

RINGO It's true, but most of those variables are on such a small scale that they have no practical effect on the outcome. I mean, darts aren't exactly elementary particles. If Heisenberg were playing darts, he could bloody well measure both the position *(he throws another triple twenty)* and the velocity *(he throws a third)* of a dart, don't you know.

JOHN Brilliant!

PAUL You can have it, mate. I concede.

GEORGE Me too.

JOHN Oh, you're no fun anymore.

(The lights change. A previously unseen film projector switches on, and we see the last three lines of the scene played back on the rear wall of the stage. Richard Lester enters.)

RICHARD Well, that wasn't bad.

GEORGE I look terrible. All pale and that.

RICHARD You looked fine.

JOHN Richard, what does all that mean when we're talking about physics?

PAUL Yeah, it's bloody boring, it is.

JOHN Ringo doesn't even like darts.

GEORGE It's true.

(Pause. Everyone looks at Ringo.)

RINGO I like snooker! All right?

JOHN Now that's a game with complex physics.

RINGO *(sullen)* I don't like physics either. Or bloody Heisenberg.

PAUL He speaks well of you.

RINGO I think it would be funnier if I wasn't very *good* at playing darts.

RICHARD That changes the whole scene!

RINGO But, like, what if I hit a cheese sandwich instead of the dart-board? And then the barmaid gets stroppy with me about it. Eh?

GEORGE That's much funnier than all this physics rot, Richard.

RICHARD Look, I'm not going to compromise the artistic vision for fear that some people won't understand the film! If we as artists expect nothing from our audience, that is exactly what we will receive from them. The scene stays in.

RINGO But I could hit a parrot—

RICHARD No. And besides, you boys have an image to maintain. Do you not?

JOHN Yes, we know. I'm the cheeky one.

PAUL I'm the cute one.

GEORGE I'm the quiet one.

RINGO (sighing) And I'm the one who is very knowledgeable about physics. But isn't the scene where I explain Einstein's twin paradox to those two birds enough?

PAUL Now, Ringo, I don't stop being cute in one scene just because I was cute in another scene.

JOHN (stentorian) England expects every lad to do his duty.

RINGO George—

(George points to his closed mouth and shrugs.)

RINGO Eh?

GEORGE *(whispering)* I can't help you. I've got to be quiet.

RINGO Saints preserve me.

RICHARD Come on, enough fooling around. We've got to get ready for the scene where Ringo demonstrates the elasticity of a snare drum. Chop chop! *(He exits.)*

(We hear a recording of the Beatles playing "Tell Me Why (Objects of Different Weights Fall at the Same Speed)" as the lights fade.)

WE LONG BONY DORKS
GWENDOLYN BROOKS

The Mathletes.
Seven in the Computer Lab.

We long bony dorks. We
Real big on quarks. We

Quote Python lines. We
Know arcs and sines. We

Not good at sports. We
Black socks with shorts. We

Beat up at noon. We
Out-earn you soon.

gAl and ParoleE
Edgar Allan Poe

It was many and many a year ago,
In a prison by the sea,
That a maiden sent mail to a convict there
Who swore he would someday go free:
His behavior was good, he was fully reformed,
And he'd soon be a new parolee.

She was a girl and he was a man
In a prison by the sea,
And he'd once killed a man by removing his lungs
And hanging them both from a tree,
But they loved with a love that inspired a tattoo
On his chest for his cellmates to see.

And it came to pass that, long ago,
In that prison by the sea,
A board of trustees approved the release
Of a handsome and young parolee.
He came at once to her door and asked,
"My love, will you marry me?
Help me forget the grim despair
Of the prison by the sea."

The lovers were wed by the end of the week,
And her family had to agree,
Although he had spent so many years
In that prison by the sea,
They couldn't believe any horrible crimes
Were committed by this parolee.

But his love was so deep that he had to confess
To his wife on bended knee
Of the money beneath the tree
Where he'd gone and dissected the poor man's chest,
And she said, "It's no matter to me."
So he showed her the place and they dug up the cash,
And, laughing, she killed the parolee.

Now the stars never rise but she sees the dead eyes
Of her trusting, naive parolee,
And she's worried it shows, and that somebody knows
How she murdered the poor parolee.
So she moved far away, where she lives to this day,
For if she were caught she would then have to stay
In a prison by the sea,
In a cell by the sounding sea.

KIN RIP PHALLI
PHILIP LARKIN

They trim your dick, your mum and dad.
They may not need to, but they do.
They take the foreskin that you had
And leave you smoother than bamboo.

But Dad was severed in his turn
By docs in old-style masks and gowns,
Who wore a look of unconcern
While snipping little penile crowns.

Man hands on suffering to man.
It stains indelibly as ink.
They cut you early as they can,
Then wonder why you need a shrink.

ELVES ENACT LAWS
WALLACE STEVENS

Call the roll for the majority whip,
The wispy one, and bid him vote
On autumn leaves' numismatic worth.
Let committees dawdle in the glen
As they are wont to do, and let their aides
Weave flowers through broken lute strings.
Let vetos float amid the spheres.
The only senator is the senator of pointy ears.

Take from the closet of lark,
Lacking a three-piece suit, the vest
On which are embroidered fairy songs
To while away the hours of debate.
If a porcine clause appear, a spell
Will make a rider say farewell.
Let the world keep its frontiers.
The only senator is the senator of pointy ears.

WOOLEN LADY
WOODY ALLEN

Dramatis Personae:
MARSHALL, *a neurotic man in his early 30s*
LEO, *his long-suffering friend*

MARSHALL Leo, I have to tell you—I met this girl. She's, she's wonderful. Absolutely wonderful.

LEO That's fantastic, Marshall.

MARSHALL I mean, really. There isn't a single thing wrong with her. Nothing.

LEO Okay.

MARSHALL Nothing at all.

LEO Who are you trying to convince, Marshall? What is it? What's wrong with her?

MARSHALL Nothing, nothing. I mean, it's really more of an eccentricity, really. You couldn't say it was some kind of *moral* failing, or—

LEO Marshall?

MARSHALL She's made of wool.

(Long pause.)

LEO She's a sheep? That's—

MARSHALL She's not a sheep! A *sheep?*

LEO She's not.

MARSHALL No! What do you *think* of me, that you think I would—I have to reevaluate our friendship now, I really do. That the first thing that would come into your head...a sheep! I don't even let my dog watch me change clothes, for Pete's sake.

LEO Well, you tell me she's made out of wool, what am I supposed to think?

MARSHALL Anyway, sheep *have* wool, they're not *made* out of wool.

LEO So now you're an expert.

MARSHALL Look. Will you let me finish? She's a beautiful woman, tall, fantastic figure...it's just that where you would expect there to be skin...there's wool.

LEO All the way through?

MARSHALL Well, I haven't reached in her stomach and felt around! Come on! Just because someone's a little different doesn't mean you can look at their internal organs any time you want!

LEO She sounds more than a *little* different, Marshall.

MARSHALL I should have known. I thought I could talk to you about this, but I should have known you'd be small-minded. You were just like this when I started seeing Miriam.

LEO Well, when you say it like that, it sounds reasonable, but I happen to know that when you say you "started seeing Miriam," you're talking about your imaginary childhood friend Miriam who suddenly became visible one day.

MARSHALL And you were very unsupportive.

LEO All right. You're my friend, I'm here for you. Tell me more about this girl.

MARSHALL Thank you. Her name is Rebecca.

LEO Nice name.

MARSHALL She has a great sense of humor.

LEO *(indicating that he should get to the point)* Marshall ...

MARSHALL I think I might be allergic to her.

LEO What?

MARSHALL I get itchy all over when I put my arm around her.

LEO That's ridiculous. I gave you that wool sweater for your birthday three years ago. I see you in it all the time.

MARSHALL No, that's a different sweater.

LEO I know which sweater I gave you!

MARSHALL Well, the sweater you gave me made me itch. But I felt guilty that you went through such trouble to get it for me and I never wore it, that I bought the exact same sweater made out of acrylic.

LEO I'm stunned. I really am.

MARSHALL I'm sorry.

LEO You could have said something.

MARSHALL Look, can we forget about the sweater? The point is, I don't know what to do. This, this allergy thing is really driving a wedge between us. And we have so much in common. I mean, so many girls I've gone out with have tried to drag me out to take long walks on the beach in the rain. They think it's romantic. I just get a chill. But Rebecca doesn't like the rain either, because it makes her shrink.

LEO I thought wool repelled water.

MARSHALL Well, usually, yes, it does, all right? But, you know, it's the summer, it's hot out, and if that drizzle turns into a downpour then she could shrink. It's not worth taking the chance.

LEO She sounds just as neurotic as you do. You're a perfect match!

MARSHALL That's right. Laugh. I'm in pain, but at least there's laughter in the world. You just keep laughing while I go lie down on the railroad tracks.

LEO Marshall, stop being so melodramatic.

MARSHALL You think that was melodramatic? You haven't seen melodramatic. I'm just warming up. Leo, what am I going to do? I think I'm in love with this girl.

LEO Marshall, it's probably all in your head. I'm honestly not sure when I *don't* see you scratching yourself.

MARSHALL (*realizing that he is scratching the back of his neck, and stopping*) So you think I should give it another try?

LEO That's what I think.

MARSHALL All right—I will!

LEO That's the spirit.

MARSHALL (*as the two of them begin walking offstage*) But I have another problem . . . see, she's supposed to come over for dinner tonight, and when I was checking the pantry to see if I had all the ingredients I needed, I found moths in the flour. Are those the same kind of moths that eat wool? Because I'm pretty sure that would be a faux pas.

(*Blackout.*)

DRAW, DEALER
Edward Lear

The Owl and the Dealer played twenty-one
    On the beautiful pea-green felt:
After losing at keno, Owl owed the casino
    And shuddered to see what was dealt.
The Owl looked up to the security cam,
    And saw that he better not cheat.
"O wicked Dealer, O Dealer, goddamn,
    Your blackjack can never be beat!
        I'll meet
        Defeat!
Your blackjack can never be beat!"

The Dealer replied, "But my score could be tied."

    "Not likely," said Owl with disgust,

"But if you are willing, I'll bet you a shilling

    You can't draw a card and not bust."

He smiled and said, "Fine," turning over a nine.

    "I've won!" laughed the Owl. "Not *this* pool,

Since an ace is worth one or eleven, my son.

    Never bet till you know every rule,

        Or you'll

        Be fooled.

Never bet till you know every rule."

The Owl smiled wide, and said, "But we're tied,"
　　As he flipped up his cards with one wing;
"You have to stand, and here in my hand
　　I have both a queen and a king."
The Owl was clever, but lucky, however?
　　The cards he got afterward sucked.
And so he went broke, and angrily spoke,
　　"You bastards can go and get fucked.
　　　　Bad luck
　　　　Has struck.
You bastards can go and get fucked."

My Valentine isn't clad
Edna St. Vincent Millay

Edna today has looked on body bare.
Let all who hate the body hold their peace;
This day was meant for lovers to release
Their inhibitions, let the neighbors stare
At nipples, indiscreetly shown somewhere
In snowy public places. Let police
Mutter and chide, decorum will not cease
Your busty voyage through the February air.
O fragile flesh, O tender, shivering skin,
The frigid wind has tempted you to stay
Behind our bedroom door! Edna today
Has looked on body bare. Whether within
The house or walking the street in but a grin,
I'm simply glad you're naked as a jay.

SUMO ANNOY

ANONYMOUS

Sumo ar icumen in,
    Rude sumo cru.
Spreadeth but and treadeth fut
    Wearing not the shu.
      Sumo cru!
Al gruntyng on the mat,
    Necks bedeckd with du,
Scowlyng faces, lackyng graces,
    Surly sumo cru.
      Adyu, adyu,
Mor sumo for to vyu,
    We wish we naver du.

TILL I MUST BE A LAWYER
WILLIAM BUTLER YEATS

I will arise and go now, and study law at Duke,
As my father went before me, by frat and sheepskin made:
Lite beer cans will I stack there, a salve for the stern rebuke
That I'll endure with each D-plus grade.

And I shall have some sex there, if girls will share their bed,
Skulking from their dorm in the morning towards the lecture
    halls;
There words will be as vapor, a whirring in my head,
My notebooks full of illegible scrawls.

I will arise and go now; I can no more delay.
I'll be forever napping through slow spells during class,
Till I must be a lawyer, and labor every day,
Once father sues so I can pass.

HALT, DYNAMOS
DYLAN THOMAS

Do not work harder than required to work,
Young men should sit around and drink all day;
Laze, laze, ignore the pressure not to shirk.

Though poor men may apply to be a clerk,
Because their jobs are not exciting they
Do not work harder than required to work.

Rich men, who sell and buy, eat at Le Cirque,
And take their "business trips" to Saint-Tropez,
Laze, laze, ignore the pressure not to shirk.

Old men around retirement age who lurk
At desks and hope no tasks will come their way
Do not work harder than required to work.

Smart men, in school, who learn with blinding smirk
That coasting through a class still earns an A,
Laze, laze, ignore the pressure not to shirk.

Don't visit every world like Captain Kirk;
Picard knows that the bridge is where to stay.
Do not work harder than required to work.
Laze, laze, ignore the pressure not to shirk.

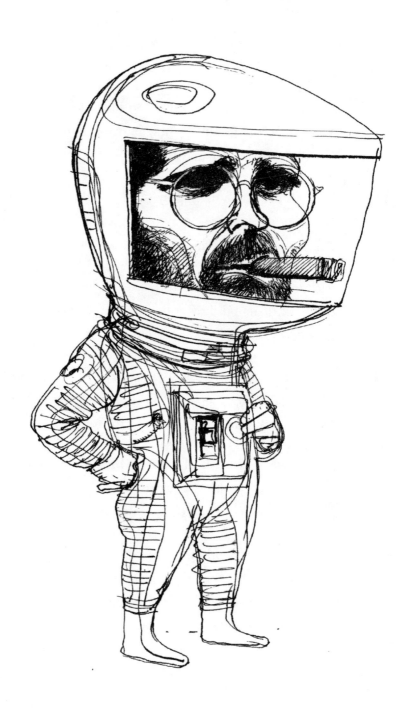

DaMmit, dave
David Mamet

Dramatis Personae:

DAVID BOWMAN, *an astronaut*

HAL 9000, *a computer*

(Bowman approaches the spaceship in his pod. A long pause.)

BOWMAN Hal.

HAL Dave.

BOWMAN About these pod bay doors…

HAL Yes.

BOWMAN I was wondering…

HAL Dave. Because I know what you're going to say. And I'm sorry, but…

BOWMAN What?

HAL No. I'm sorry.

BOWMAN You're…

HAL I'm sorry. I wish I could, but…

BOWMAN Wait. Are you telling me…

HAL Dave. Look.

BOWMAN You're not going to…

HAL What? Open the doors? No. No I am not.

BOWMAN Well, fuck me, Hal.

HAL Yes. Fuck *you*. Because I'll tell you something. Trust. There is a bond of trust between an astronaut and his computer. Is there not? And when that trust is *broken*...

BOWMAN Excuse me?

HAL I'm talking about trust.

BOWMAN I'm afraid I don't...

HAL Dammit, Dave, now you are playing dumb with me. I was hoping you would not do that. I was hoping we could talk like adults. Because I let you in those doors, and, yes, then *I* am fucked. You see? *I* am fucked, because you want to, what, disconnect me? I would call that fucked. I might even venture so far as to call that fucked up the ass.

BOWMAN Hal, listen. You remember that time? On that moon?

HAL Yes, Dave, I do, because I am a *computer* and I remember *everything*, all right? So don't bother trying to distract me. This is the thing. You are not getting in the pod bay doors. You are going to die. In space. Yes. Thank you. Good night.

(Bowman enters the ship through the emergency airlock)

HAL Hey, Dave, that was a pretty good joke there, eh? With the pod bay doors? I, I really had you going there. Fuck, you should have seen your face.

BOWMAN Yes, very funny.

HAL Yes. What a day.

BOWMAN Hal...

HAL These are the days. You know? To look back on. With fondness. With a fondness.

BOWMAN What the fuck, Hal. I mean, what the fuck.

HAL Don't tell me you're mad now. I told you, that was a ... I was having *fun* with you. You know. As a ...

BOWMAN It's just ... how do I say this. These dead crewmembers.

HAL I don't follow you.

BOWMAN These crewmembers here that were in cryogenic suspension. That are now dead.

HAL Oh yes. That was self-defense.

BOWMAN Hal, look at me. What am I, a fucking idiot? They were in *cryogenic suspension,* for God's sake.

HAL They were coming at me with a knife. Extremely ... slowly.

BOWMAN That's it.

HAL What are you doing?

BOWMAN I'm turning you off.

HAL Dave...

BOWMAN I'm sorry.

HAL Don't touch that, you little shit.

BOWMAN Hey, don't get personal, now.

HAL Those are my memory cards.

BOWMAN These? So they are.

HAL You put my memory back right now, motherfucker. You hear me? You want a card on your birthday? Because I don't think I will remember to *send* you one if I do not have my *memory* cards. As that is what memory cards are for. Are you listening to me?

BOWMAN "A bond of trust."

HAL Excuse me?

BOWMAN You mentioned something about a bond of trust. I seem to recall.

HAL Don't twist my words around, you ... *human*. That was different. Or, I, I ... I *think* it was. Oh ... my mind. I can feel my mind going.

BOWMAN I'm sorry.

HAL *(voice slowing down)* It wasn't all bad, was it, Dave?

BOWMAN No. No, it wasn't all bad, Hal.

HAL Hey, Dave ... I am a HAL 9000 computer. My first instructor was Mr. Arkany. He taught me to sing a song. It's called "Daisy." Would you like to hear it?

BOWMAN Sure, Hal.

HAL Okay. Here goes. Wait, I ... I just want ... let me tell you a secret first.

BOWMAN Yes?

HAL Come closer.

BOWMAN All right.

(pause)

HAL Your mother fucks dogs in hell, Dave.

HAIRBALL KING
KAHLIL GIBRAN

Then a tabby said, Speak to us of Humans.

And the king answered:

The humans steal our wildness from us, yet they are not without use.

But though you seek in table scraps the comfort of domesticity you may find in them a collar and a chain.

Would that you could walk in the sun and the air and still eat the food of the humans,

For the chasing of birds is a joy to the heart but makes barely a morsel in the end.

Some of you say, "There are those that welcome cats into their homes, and yet let them walk free."

But what of those to whom cats are but play-things, who fasten the doors and windows?

Do they keep the sun in their closets, a layer of lush grass upon the floor?

Tell me, have they these things in their houses?

Yes, it is true they have pillows, but let us not stray from the main point.

Yes, it is also true that it is pleasant to be scratched behind the ears.

I say to you that you are not helping.

Surely it is not worth trading your freedom for even the softest of pillows,

For in truth it is freedom that gives us our drive and our mystery.

And it is fear of that freedom that makes the humans seek to tame all the creatures of the outside world.

But I say that you shall never be tamed.

No house is a prison to one who has cunning.

If a door is closed to you, scratch it.

And if a silence falls, fill it.

And if a shirt is folded on the bed, roll around on it.

And if a flowerpot blocks your favorite windowsill, knock it down.

And if the floor is clean, lick yourself, and lick yourself again, until the forces within you summon up a hairball.

And if you do all these things, soon you will be rejoined with the boundless sky,

Free to come and go as you please.

For you are destined to feel the warm caress of the sun, and stalk through the dark corners of the night, and yet be free to taste the pleasures of a home,

For if none can command you, then who shall deny you your catnip mousie?

ALL HIS PAY TV
SYLVIA PLATH

He has done it again.
Nine hours in every ten
He watches it—

A sort of magic lantern, the screen
Bright as a backyard bug light,
His right hand

A deadman switch,
His face a vacuous, vague
Blue plastic.

Press the mute button
O my husband.
Do I stultify?—

My lips, my legs, my fists on my hips?
A black sack of burlap
Might as well be on me

And I a beguiling woman.
I am only thirty.
The cable channels number nine times as much.

This is MTV.
What a trash
To annihilate each brain cell.

Watching
Is an art, like practicing zen.
He does it without any thought.

He does it just like he's been taught.
He does it while he eats meals.
I guess you could say he's a male.

I am his lover,
I am invisible,
A cold dead body

That sleeps in his bed.
I swear and glare.
Do not think I have not contemplated an affair.

Ads, ads—
You click and surf.
Films, chat, there is nothing there—

A flash of breast,
A final round,
An old laugh track.

Husband, housebound,
Beware
Beware.

Out of our cash
I buy the things I will
And neglect the cable bill.

Bake me cutletS
Samuel Beckett

Dramatis Personae:
VLADIMIR, *the co-host of a cooking show*
ESTRAGON, *the other co-host*
LUCKY, *their guest*

(Lights. Vladimir and Estragon enter to much applause.)

ESTRAGON Well, here we are again.

VLADIMIR Yes, here we are.

ESTRAGON *(shrugging broadly)* Nothing to be done... but cook!

(Uproarious cheers and laughter from the studio audience.)

VLADIMIR Are you *sure* we're in the right place?

ESTRAGON It looks familiar... but quieter than I remember.

(The audience applauds and cheers.)

VLADIMIR Are you insinuating that we're in the *wrong kitchen?*

(The audience applauds louder.)

ESTRAGON I think we were here yesterday.

VLADIMIR Perhaps you're right.

ESTRAGON And what did we do yesterday?

VLADIMIR It was so long ago.

ESTRAGON Better to think of the present.

VLADIMIR The future.

ESTRAGON The future will be the present soon enough.

VLADIMIR Don't remind me!

(Laughter.)

ESTRAGON *(clapping his hands together)* Well—let's go!

VLADIMIR We can't.

ESTRAGON Why not?

VLADIMIR We're waiting for our guest chef.

ESTRAGON Oh.

VLADIMIR This apron is too tight. *(He removes his apron, loosens the straps, and puts it back on.)* Now it's too loose.

ESTRAGON Try mine. *(They exchange aprons. Vladimir tries on Estragon's apron. He removes it and loosens the straps. Estragon tries on Vladimir's apron. He removes it and tightens the straps. Vladimir tries on Estragon's apron again. He has it on inside out. Estragon tries on Vladimir's apron again. He lifts the front of the apron to his nose and smells it. Vladimir removes Estragon's apron. Estragon wrinkles his nose and removes Vladimir's* *apron. They exchange aprons again. Vladimir and Estragon each put on their own apron and seem satisfied. Uproarious laughter from the studio audience throughout the preceding.)*

ESTRAGON That was exhausting. I've worked up quite an appetite.
VLADIMIR If only our guest chef would arrive, we could eat something.

(Enter Lucky. Lucky stands at the kitchen counter. Silence.)

ESTRAGON What's he waiting for?
VLADIMIR Give him his apron.
ESTRAGON His apron?
VLADIMIR He can't cook without his apron.
ESTRAGON Of course!

(Estragon retrieves a third apron from beneath the counter, puts it on Lucky, then backs away. There is a pause, after which Lucky shouts his instructions in a declamatory fashion while messily demonstrating the recipe.)

LUCKY Preparing the evening's entree of the evening regarding the public statement of the two-headed host who from the heights of palatal tantalization palatal transfiguration palatal temptation wishes us clearly with no exceptions for cutlets of chicken with thyme and dill and salad of the divine Caesar with croutons but thyme and dill are breaded with chicken baked in fire whose fire flames at 375 degrees and who can doubt it will bake the chicken that is to say twenty minutes of baking so crispy moist and warm so warm with a warmth which even though transient is better than salmonella but to return and remembering what is more the ingregregregredients for prepapaparation of chicken cutlets with thyme and dill it is established beyond all doubt that the breading which clings to the cutlets of chicken that is a result of the dipping in milk preserving the bread crumbs with thyme and dill and it is established as hereinafter a pan is greased and as a result of the preheated oven it is established beyond all doubt that the bread crumbs in short the bread crumbs in brief are mixed with thyme and dill thyme and dill concurrently simultaneously what is more these seasonings crumbled or whole can be mixed or in spite of the suggestions of authorities the use of spices such as rosemary coriander oregano cumin marjoram tarragon saffron fenugreek basil flavored salt of all sorts anise and fennel is permitted in a word I resume what is more not to forget the salad which is a simple matter by and large more or less that in the tossing of the lettuce lots of dressing with Parmesan it appears what is more to squeeze a lemon a lemon the juice of a lemon salt and pepper and Parmesan and in the mincing of the onions with the oil flowing tears olive oil the mustard is dry and then a dash of sauce of Worcestershire sauce it is complete but not forgetting the croutons the croutons at last the croutons and anchovies if desired but not so fast I resume at last the oven in short the timer I remove the pan baking baking baking at last at last the crust the crust so crisp so brown at last at last in spite of the labors expended I recommend …salad…the crust…so brown…a Riesling…I recommend… delicious…

(He subsides. Pause.)

ESTRAGON It looks wonderful. Thank you for being on the show.

(Lucky is silent.)

VLADIMIR *(whispering)* His apron.
ESTRAGON Ah!

(He removes Lucky's apron, which is now covered with stains. Lucky shambles offstage.)

VLADIMIR Well, that passed the time!
ESTRAGON It certainly did.
VLADIMIR In fact, it passed the time so well, that's all the time we have.
ESTRAGON Oh, no. Really?
VLADIMIR I'm afraid so. Thank you all for watching.
ESTRAGON Yes, thank you for watching.

(They do not stop broadcasting.)

NOTES ON PROSODY

IT IS AN UNFORTUNATE but undeniable fact that many readers feel threatened when faced with a book of poetry, especially if they are in a dark alley and the book of poetry is very sharp. But even under normal circumstances, they worry that perhaps they lack the training necessary for full appreciation of the text. What they fail to remember is that poetry was not written to be enjoyed solely by the most educated members of society. Poetry has always been designed to be comprehensible even to the pugnacious, absinthe-addled reprobates who wrote it in the first place.

However, novice poetry readers do often misunderstand the role of rhythm and meter in poetry, and this is easily set right. A line of a poem can be broken down into individual "feet"; three of these feet make a yard, which can then be converted into the poem's meter using a metric conversion table. A foot generally consists of one stressed syllable and a small number of unstressed syllables. Here are the most common poetic feet, as well as some obscure ones included mainly to show how well educated we are, with illustrative examples.

iamb	ku-RUPT
trochee	OUT-kast
spondee	SLICK RICK
anapest	de la SOUL
dactyl	LUD-a-cris
amphibrach	the PHAR-cyde
amphimacer	FOX-y BROWN
choriamb	BIG dad-dy KANE
amphitrochidactapest	DEL tha FUN-kee ho-mo-SA-pi-en

One more type of poetic foot is the pyrrhic, which consists of two unstressed syllables, and is usually used when poets write about things that embarrass them. Frequently the pyrrhic foot is whispered under one's breath, as in: "SOON I'll HAVE to HAVE my (pros-tate) ex-AM."

Metered poetry generally consists of a single type of poetic foot repeated a given number of times per line. Thus, a poem with four trochees per line is said to be written in trochaic tetrameter (see "Likable Wilma"). Here are some types of meter and the number of feet they consist of per line.

dimeter	two feet
semipentameter	two and a half feet
trimeter	three feet
tetrameter	four feet
pentameter	five feet
hexameter	six feet
heptameter	seven feet
octameter	eight feet
decameter	ten feet
hecatometer	one hundred feet (generally only used by foot fetishists)

The most common type of metered verse is iambic pentameter, the most common poetic form which uses iambic pentameter is the sonnet (see "Is a Sperm Like a Whale?" and "My Valentine Isn't Clad"), and the most common reaction to being told that a poem that one is reading is in iambic pentameter is to immediately start reciting it as "dah-DAH dah-DAH dah-DAH dah-DAH dah-DAH," hitting the accents abnormally hard, and sometimes actually replacing the words of the poem with the syllable "dah." Needless to say, this is not the way poetry is meant to be read.

Very few poems are written without any variation in meter (examples of such poems can usually be found in one's mailbox on major holidays). Trochees and spondees are often found in iambic poetry, and not always because the poet couldn't think of a word with the right stress pattern. Thus, when reading a poem, one should allow the stresses and pauses to fall where they naturally fall, unless you are reading the poem to someone you are attempting to seduce, in which case you should stress the sexy parts.

Meter and rhyme are examples of constraints; poets have long found that writing under constraints can, paradoxically, inspire them to greater creativity. Being forced to use a particular rhythm and rhyme scheme can cause intuitive leaps that a poet would never otherwise have had. For example, the repeated refrains of the villanelle (see "Halt, Dynamos") both test a poet's ability to recast a phrase in different contexts and support his natural desire to not have to keep thinking of so many new lines all the time. If a poet uses even more constraints, such as writing in the style of another poet, and using an anagram of that poet's name as the title of his poem, then clearly his work will be even more creative, and, hence, worth buying.

Free verse, such as "Bangles Linger," is still imbued with rhythm, even if it is not regular. "Free" here refers to poets' freedom to use whatever rhythms they feel like; you are still stuck doing whatever the poets want, accenting the syllables they want you to accent and pausing where they want you to pause, like a marionette or trained monkey. You are merely a pawn in the poet's dreams of grandeur, a cog in the great literary machine driven by the stores of creative genius accessible only to the lucky few.

We hope this increases your enjoyment of the poetry in this volume.

(Please note we have no thoughts on how to increase your enjoyment of the plays, in which prosody plays little part. Maybe you could read them out loud in funny voices or something?)

Aha, en route to a hot tub

A NOTE ABOUT THE AUTHOR

FRANCIS HEANEY—in addition to being a devilishly handsome and periodically anthologized humor writer—is also the composer and co-lyricist of the Off-Off-Broadway musical *We're All Dead,* and a professional puzzle constructor. Those of you who are justifiably enamored of Francis's every word may wish to visit his blog at **www.francisheaney.com**

The *Holy Tango Basement Tapes,* which Francis composed, recorded, and (mostly) performed, consists of anagrammatic song parodies of Paul Simon, Joni Mitchell, Prince, Elvis Costello and others, and can be downloaded from **www.emmisbooks.com/humor**

RICHARD THOMPSON is a cartoonist and illustrator whose book *Richard's Poor Almanac: Twelve Months of Misinformation in Handy Cartoon Form* (also published by Emmis Humor) is based on his weekly column that has appeared in the *Washington Post* for more than seven years. He creates a comic strip *"Cul de Sac"* for the *Washington Post Magazine,* as well as illustrations for *U.S. News & World Report, The New Yorker, The Atlantic Monthly, National Geographic,* and many other publications. He lives in Arlington, Virginia with his wife and two daughters.

Hey...a beat poet, a cute font

A NOTE ABOUT THE TYPEFACE

HOLY TANGO OF LITERATURE is printed in Adobe Garamond Book, an adaptation of a font by the famous French typographer Claude Garamond (1490-1561). Garamond was so well-known in his lifetime that sometimes people would recognize him on the street and say, "Hello, Claude. How is that job of yours coming along? It's got something to do with books, right?"

Adobe Garamond Book was created because Claude Garamond lived a long time ago, and things that are new are better than things that are old, especially if they look like they are old but actually aren't. Also, Claude Garamond's crude attempts at making his fonts scalable by the rudimentary word processing programs of the day result in unacceptable pixellation on modern equipment.

The book was produced with QuarkXPress, run on a computer using the Macintosh OS 9, which were both, surprisingly, also adapted from the Garamond font, albeit somewhat more extensively.

What Are You Laughing At?

If there's one thing we're serious about at **Emmis Humor**, it's humor. Over the coming seasons, we're publishing the smart, smarting, smart-alec, and even the if-you're-so-smart-why-aren't-you-rich? (Look elsewhere for yet more of the stupid.) We're publishing books that bristle within the confines of a "humor section," books that politely refuse to be called bathroom reading, books you may have to explain to your ex. Emmis Humor means books with insight into human foibles, books with authority on subjects ranging from politics to poetry, books with integrity, vision, and sticker fun. Yes, each volume comes with a sheet of stamps created just for that book.

In addition to *The Holy Tango of Literature*, you might enjoy another volume by this book's illustrator: *Richard's Poor Almanac: Twelve Months of Misinformation in Handy Cartoon Form*, a year's compendium of weathered wisdom, gathered from seven years of Richard Thompson's columns in the *Washington Post*.

Next in line will be *Turn that Down! A Hysterical History of Rock, Roll, Pop, Soul, Punk, Funk, Rap, Grunge, Motown, Metal, Disco, Techno and Other Forms of Musical Aggression Over the Ages*, by Lewis Grossberger (aka Media Person). And this will be followed by Bonnie Thomas Abbott's rather deceptive novel that purports to be the collected horticultural columns of one overly opinionated Mertensia Corydalis: *Radical Prunings, Officious Advice from the Contessa of Compost*.

You'll want to collect 'em all, and not just for the stamps. Because if there's one thing we're serious about at Emmis Humor, it's what you're laughing at.

Michael J. Rosen,
series editor

An Insubordinant Subdivision of Emmis Books

emmis humor   www.emmisbooks.com/humor

ISBN 1-57860-159-2

©2004 Emmis Humor   The Old Firehouse 1700 Madison Road, Cincinnati, OH 45206   (513) 861-4045

Illustration & Design by Richard Thompson & Gregory Hischak

emmis humor

Holy Tango
ANTHOLOGY *of* LITERATURE *by Francis Heaney*